Pebble® Plus

Look Inside Animal Homes
Look Inside a Bee Hive

by Megan Cooley Peterson

Consulting Editor: Gail Saunders-Smith, PhD

Consultant: Tom Seeley
Professor of Neurobiology and Behavior
Cornell University
Ithaca, New York

CAPSTONE PRESS
a capstone imprint

Pebble Plus is published by Capstone Press,
151 Good Counsel Drive, P.O. Box 669, Mankato, Minnesota 56002.
www.capstonepub.com

 Books published by Capstone Press are manufactured with paper
containing at least 10 percent post-consumer waste.

Library of Congress Cataloging-in-Publication Data
Peterson, Megan Cooley.
 Look inside a bee hive / by Megan Cooley Peterson.
   p. cm.—(Pebble plus. Look inside animal homes)
 Includes bibliographical references and index.
 Summary: "Full-color photographs and simple text describe bee hives"—Provided by publisher.
 ISBN 978-1-4296-6075-4 (library binding)
 1. Bees—Habitations—Juvenile literature. 2. Beehives—Juvenile literature. I. Title.
 QL565.2.P48 2012
 595.79'9—dc22   2011000264

Editorial Credits
Katy Kudela, editor; Gene Bentdahl, designer; Marcie Spence, media researcher; Laura Manthe, production specialist

Photo Credits
Ardea: Steve Hopkin, 9; iStockphoto: alamostudios, 11, picturethatphoto, 15; Minden Pictures: Gerry Ellis, 19,
Heidi & Hans-Juergen Koch, 21, S & D & K Maslowski, 7, Stephen Dalton, 17; Photolibrary/Peter Arnold, Inc.:
John Brown, 13; Shutterstock: Mircea Bezergheanu, cover, 5, Tischenko Irina, 1

Note to Parents and Teachers

The Look Inside Animal Homes series supports national science standards related to life
science. This book describes and illustrates honey bee hives. The images support early readers
in understanding the text. The repetition of words and phrases helps early readers learn new
words. This book also introduces early readers to subject-specific vocabulary words, which are
defined in the Glossary section. Early readers may need assistance to read some words and to
use the Table of Contents, Glossary, Read More, Internet Sites, and Index sections of the book.

Printed in the United States of America in North Mankato, Minnesota.
032011   006110CGF11

Table of Contents

A Home for Honey Bees

Honey bees live in hives
all year long.
As many as 60,000 bees
live in one hive.

Building a Honey Bee Hive

Worker bees build a hive

in about six weeks.

They first find a hollow tree

in a forest or town.

The tree keeps the hive safe.

Worker bees then build

a set of wax combs

inside the tree.

Bees make wax

inside their bodies.

Worker bees shape wax
into rows of cells. Each cell
is a small room with six sides.
Bees build 100,000 cells
in a hive.

Inside a Honey Bee Hive

A small hole in the tree

lets honey bees buzz

into the hive.

Guard bees sting any enemies

that try to enter.

The queen bee lays eggs
in the center part of the combs.
Each cell holds one egg.
She lays up to 2,000 eggs
each day.

queen bee

Worker bees store pollen

in cells near the eggs.

They feed pollen

to the baby bees.

pollen

Worker bees turn nectar

into honey.

They store honey

at the top of the combs.

By late spring the hive
is too small for all the bees.
Some bees leave the hive.
They will build a new hive
before winter.

Glossary

cell—a small section in the comb of a hive

comb—a group of wax cells built by worker bees inside their hives; bees store pollen, honey, and eggs in the cells of a comb

hive—a structure where a colony of bees lives, such as a hollow tree or a wooden box

hollow—empty inside

nectar—a sweet liquid found in many flowers

pollen—tiny yellow grains in flowers

queen bee—an adult female bee that lays eggs; only one queen lives in a hive

wax—a yellow substance made by bees and used to build combs

worker bee—an adult female bee that does not lay eggs; worker bees build combs and take care of young bees

Read More

Mortensen, Lori. *In the Trees, Honey Bees.* Sharing Nature with Children. Nevada City, Calif.: Dawn Publications, 2009.

Rotner, Shelley. *The Buzz on Bees: Why Are They Disappearing?* New York: Holiday House, 2010.

Internet Sites

FactHound offers a safe, fun way to find Internet sites related to this book. All of the sites on FactHound have been researched by our staff.

Here's all you do:

Visit *www.facthound.com*

Type in this code: 9781429660754

Super-cool stuff! Check out projects, games and lots more at www.capstonekids.com

Index

Word Count: 188
Grade: 1
Early-Intervention Level: 15